THE BOTTOMLESS CLOUD

How AI, the next generation of the cloud, and abundance thinking will radically transform the way you do business.

Thomas Koulopoulos, CEO Delphi Group
David Friend, CEO Wasabi
DelphiGroup.com | Wasabi.com
TheBottomlessCloud.com

HybridGlobal
PUBLISHING

Published by
Hybrid Global Publishing
301 E 57th Street, 4th fl
New York, NY 10022

Manufactured in the United States of America, or in the United Kingdom when distributed elsewhere.

Koulopoulos, Thomas
  The Bottomless Cloud: How AI, the next generation of the cloud, and abundance thinking will radically transform the way you do business
  ISBN: 978-1-948181-38-9

Cover design by: Joe Potter / joepotter.com
Interior design: Claudia Volkman

tkspeaks.com
delphigroup.com
wasabi.com
thebottomlesscloud.com

*We consistently fail
to grasp how many
ideas remain to be discovered . . .*

*The difficulty is the
same one we have
with compounding.*

Possibilities do not add up.

They multiply.

—Paul Romer, Nobel Prize Winning Economist

CONTENTS

INTRODUCTION

It's human nature to try and understand the future by using the lens of the past; it's what we know and what we are comfortable with. Yet, history has shown us that the future is usually far stranger than anything we can predict.

In fact, even when we can predict the trajectory of technology, we still fall far short of getting the future right.

In 1993 AT&T ran a series of ads called the You Will campaign. The ads were beyond prescient, showing GPS, tablet computing, online meetings, even streaming video that was eerily similar to Netflix. And yet AT&T didn't bring a single one of these technologies to the market. AT&T isn't alone. Kodak invented digital photography and still it was bankrupted because it held on to film emulsion technology well after the market for digital photography took off. Blockbuster turned down the opportunity to purchase its nascent rival Netflix in 2000 for a paltry $50 million. These companies saw the future but were not able to capitalize on it.

In each case what drove these technologies faster than was expected at the time were the unforeseen synergies that resulted from dramatic increases in affordability and connectivity, coupled with equally dramatic increases in the volume of data they created. Affordability and connectivity accelerated the creation of data, which then fueled the proliferation of new technologies, products, and applications, a cycle that has repeated and accelerated countless times.

This Cambrian explosion of technologies and data has changed how we live, work, and play in ways that took most people by surprise. Consider that ten years ago it would have been laughable to think that we would be carrying terabytes of data in our pockets and purses, much less that we would be accessing zettabytes (one billion terabytes) of data in the Cloud. And yet we have barely begun to experience the deluge of data that will fuel the future.

We know it may seem old hat to talk about the data avalanche. After all, isn't that what we've been experiencing since the dawn of digital computing in the 1960s? Yes, but the last 60 years are barely the first act of the prelude to what's coming. By the end of this century we will be surrounded by 10^{21} user computing devices; that's 100 times as many computing devices, collecting and creating data, as there are grains of sand on all the world's beaches.

That may seem unfathomable, yet, as with AT&T's You Will ads, technology is

> By the end of this century we will be surrounded by 100 times as many devices collecting and processing data than there are grains of sand on all the world's beaches.

easy to project; the hard part is figuring out how all of this data will create new sources of value.

The biggest challenge in understanding how data will transform our businesses and society is the industrial era lens of scarcity that we use to see the future. From Henry Ford's moving assembly lines to Westinghouse's power distribution, every aspect of how industrialization operated, managed, and measured value came down to the economics of scarcity, which could be summed up as "Keep only what's needed and get rid of everything else." Great companies optimized scarce resources, raw materials, and commodities in order to minimize costs.

That same thinking has governed our approach to data. Store only what's needed. Archive the rest. And destroy anything that does not have direct value to the business. But data isn't finite; it has no expiration date other than the artificial constraints we impose on it. It has value that can be mined long after it's created. Body cam footage is destroyed after weeks or months while the statute of limitations can last for years. Scientific data which may hold clues to the cures for deadly diseases is archived and effectively rendered inaccessible.

At the same time advances in artificial intelligence and machine learning promise to help us solve challenges which industrial era approaches simply cannot take on. For example, consider that if we continue to deliver human-driven automobiles to transport the projected increases in global population we will reach unsustainable levels of congestion and human carnage. In the USA alone we will double the total number of vehicles on the road from 240 million today to over 560 million by 2035. Globally, yearly deaths due to automobiles would increase five-fold to about 7,000,000.

AI-powered cars will reduce total vehicles by 2050 to less than 10% of the vehicles on the road today, while also reducing automobile related deaths to just 2% of the 7,000,000 projected at the current rate of human-driven car proliferation.

However, AI is fueled by massive amounts of data. So much so, that storing the amount of data needed to operate a fully autonomous automobile would cost 10 times as much as the car.

The transition to autonomous and intelligent devices, and the promise of data abundance, is only possible with the dramatic changes that we are projecting in this book. Changes that will bring about a Bottomless Cloud that is orders of magnitude less expensive and faster than on-premises or first-generation cloud solutions.

That's the objective of this book, to change the way you think about the role of data, from a by-product of business to the fuel and raw material on which businesses of the future will be built.

We've kept it simple and straightforward, but the

projections and conclusions are no less compelling. We may not be able to predict the precise future, but we do promise to crush the lens of the past and stretch your mind to understand and embrace a world of near infinite data and the revolution it will fuel across every business, industry, and social institution.

Welcome to the Bottomless Cloud.

THE REAL REVOLUTION

Power utilities were a cornerstone of the industrial age—not just by cutting the cost of power by 80%, but by radically accelerating innovation and new business models, allowing businesses to focus on what they were best at: their products and services.

At the turn of the twentieth century, more than 98 percent of all factories were powered by water wheels or reciprocating steam engines.[1] The other two percent were just starting to experiment with a radically new form of power—electricity.

These new factories were role models for the future, creating a sea change in the economics of manufacturing. They could outperform and out-produce their peers. However, electric power was dangerous, complicated, and unreliable. It required the retooling of factories and dedicated resources, staff, facilities, time, and money. In addition, companies had to build enough capacity to power their operations at peak loads even though they typically needed far less power in the normal course of operations.

As the industrial revolution began to scale rapidly at the end of the 19th century, the need for power increased dramatically—by some estimates ten-fold from 1880 to 1910.[2] At around the same time, the first power plants capable of delivering AC power over large distances began to emerge as both Edison and Westinghouse built centralized electric utilities.

Soon the idea of moving electric power from an onsite function to one managed by a utility became a mandate, not only because it cut the overall cost of power consumption to less than 20%[3] of what it had been, but also because it spurred a flurry of innovation and new business models by allowing businesses to focus on what they were best at: their products and services. Many of the cornerstone industries of the early 1900s, such as automotive and home appliances, would have been impossible to scale up without the advent of inexpensive and easily distributed power brought on by the economies of scale in the electric utility industry.

Just as electricity powered the industrial revolution one hundred years ago, data is powering today's most valuable companies—companies like Google, Facebook, and Amazon. Even companies that make durable goods, like Tesla, could not exist without an enormous quantity of data. And just as electric power generation migrated to centralized power plants, the storage of data is moving from on-premises storage to large centralized-clouds run by companies with storage expertise.

Today it seems incomprehensible that a utility such as electricity, which is so simple to use, so prevalent in our lives, and so fundamental to our businesses, was once so radically disruptive; yet, most disruptive technologies follow a similar adoption curve. As reliance on them begins to escalate, they rapidly go from a curiosity to a mad rush of incompatible approaches.

For example, before utilities and the creation of the electric grid, each company had its own standards for power generation and distribution.

This was the advent of what we'll call Electrification 1.0, in which the first providers of electric power attempted to bundle power generation and delivery as an aside to what their core businesses were. The result was countless standards for the dynamos, motors, wiring, voltages, amperages, and machinery. Soon the costs incurred by trying to resolve these problems started to approach, and eventually exceeded, the savings of internal economies of scale. In fact, many factories began to sell power to local shopkeepers and municipalities, in an attempt to shore up an eroding financial proposition.

Ultimately, the reliance on electrification was so widespread, the threat of incompatibility such a stifling factor for innovation, and the risk of obsolete investment so great that broad-based standards emerged and industry segmentation occurred.

By 1890, the generation of electricity had begun to coalesce around two competing standards: Thomas Edison's DC current, and George Westinghouse's AC current. The battle raged until the 1920s when AC eventually won out, but DC power persisted in pockets throughout most of the 20th century.

The first generation of players that pave the road for these new technologies are often only bridges that transition us from the old to the new.

Today, as Internet giants Microsoft, Google, and Amazon battle for shares of the world's data, using their own proprietary platforms, we are again faced with incompatible emerging standards.

How Giants Fall

In the early days of electrification, companies like GE and Westinghouse not only produced the equipment for power generation, but also transformers, motors, light bulbs, radios, and home appliances that consumed electricity.

The adoption of standards unleashed an enormous wave of innovation as new companies emerged that specialized in doing parts of what Westinghouse and GE were doing. Sylvania produced light bulbs, RCA produced radios, Otis produced elevators, and so forth. While GE and Westinghouse continued to make all of these products for the next 100 years, they lost their grip on many of the markets that were emerging on the back of cheap, standardized, and ubiquitous electric power.

This is similar to what happened in the steel industry. During the 1960s, US Steel was the largest steel company in the world. Their big soot-belching plants in places like Pittsburgh dominated the market. Then Nucor came along with their new electric arc furnaces and built mini-mills that were closer to their customers and sources of supply. US Steel, with their enormous entrenched infrastructure, lost ground year after year. Burdened with the cost of maintaining their old infrastructure, they couldn't afford to compete with Nucor and they didn't want to adopt Nucor's business model to only further erode their business. Today, US Steel has been delisted from the S&P and Nucor is the largest steel company in the US.[4]

In data storage, we're seeing new companies with new technologies attack giant market leaders whose technology is now over a decade old. With the Internet owned by many competing players, it's difficult for any one or a handful of companies to control access and distribution, and it's relatively easy for customers to move data from one Cloud to another, especially considering the adoption of de facto standards, like the Amazon S3 API.

Which is why, as Microsoft, Google, Amazon, and a few others compete to be all things cloud, new companies are emerging that specialize in specific pieces of the Cloud. For example, Limelight and Fastly provide content distribution networks. Packet and Linode offer compute-in-the-Cloud, Wasabi offers storage, and File Catalyst offers file transfer acceleration.

While all three of the major cloud providers have offerings in each of these categories, the "specialist" companies are thriving as customers adopt a multi-cloud "best of breed" approach, piecing together the exact components that best serve their individualized needs.

The story of how electrification evolved applies to computing and data storage just as much as it does to nearly every disruptive technology that quickly creates value in unforeseen ways—creating   distinct competitive advantage for its providers and its users.

As with electrification, the rush to use a new technology creates a chaotic and immature, though very lucrative, marketplace that scales quickly. But the first generation of players that pave the road for these new technologies are often only the bridges that transition us from the old to the new. They make the required investments to prove the initial value of the technology, but whether it's data storage or electricity, they are not always the same companies that deliver on the longer-term promise.

For example, less than thirty years ago you would send a fax by going to your local FedEx office to use ZapMail—a proprietary precursor to commodity faxing. FedEx was effectively using proprietary methods to ride the wave of instant communication, which had enormous value to companies. But these proprietary first generation approaches typically crumble under their own weight as the technology evolves. For example, it's estimated that FedEx lost upwards of $300 million on ZapMail as the fax market standardized and finally took off.[5]

The Cloud Utility

As with the evolution of electrification, companies built proprietary approaches for data storage. But these did not scale well outside of the organization and its closest partners. Inevitably, this stifled innovation, as data interoperability became the key impediment to doing business outside of any one proprietary set of data storage standards. For example, two thirds of companies claim that data storage costs are their number one data center challenge.

... each piece of data increases in value with each new piece of data captured.

Companies such as Amazon, Microsoft, and Google were among the most affected by their own increasing demands for storage. Much like our early 20th century factories and electricity providers (i.e., Westinghouse and GE), they made the logical step of using their deep expertise in storage to defray the cost of their own data centers by providing storage as a service to their customers. That seems to be where we are with data storage in the Cloud; the first generation of cloud-based storage is growing at an astonishing rate, nearly doubling year over year. After fifty years of on-premises investment in data storage, businesses have outgrown their ability to economically store all of their data on their own.

The utility model that worked so well for electrification was also now at play with data.

As with electric utilities, the cloud has become a pervasive part of how we think about the modern enterprise. However, so much of what passes for cloud data storage is still steeped in an industrial era model of scarcity, which prioritizes data based on the high cost to store it.

As a result, half of all digital data today resides in offline or archived media. Worse yet, in many applications data is destroyed soon after it's created due to high storage costs. For example, the vast majority of body cam footage is deleted in

60 to 180 days. That's a fraction of the statute of limitations for most serious crimes. Another example is the data storage costs for one year's operation of a fully autonomous vehicle, which would cost ten times that of the vehicle.

In these, and many more examples, data is not the new oil fueling the economy of the 21st century, but, instead, the friction preventing companies and society from realizing the tremendous value of data.

But the economics of storage are changing radically.

> ... the Bottomless Cloud and near zero storage costs will spur new business models and new age of innovation that we have only started to imagine.

We picture an image of the world in which storage costs no longer impede progress. Using what we will call "the Bottomless Cloud," organizations will transition into a post-industrial era that focuses on the limitless abundance of data. By 2035 we will have access to over one yottabyte of data, that's one billion petabytes, or more than the number of stars in the visible universe. As a result, new industries will evolve. In the same way that limitless electric power ushered in one hundred years of new industries and innovation, the Bottomless Cloud and near zero storage costs will spur new business models and a new age of innovation that we have only started to imagine.

In fact, let's put this in perspective. It's been projected that the world's data centers (where all of the data that's used in the Cloud is stored) are already using 25 percent more energy yearly than all of the UK and have a carbon footprint equal to that of the entire aviation industry.[6] In Japan alone, if its data centers continue to grow at their present rate, by 2030 they will consume all of Japan's energy output.[7]

Some of the greatest contributors to the data of the next 50 years will be from industries that are incipient today. For example, it's projected that by 2035, vehicles in the USA alone will produce over 100 zettabytes of data yearly.

That's more than 100 times all digital global storage in 2017. More astonishingly, however, is the fact that if we continue on our current trajectory, we would simply run out of space to store data. By 2020 it's estimated that the world will produce forty-four zettabytes (that's a 44 followed by 21 zeros) of data yearly. By 2025 that will have exploded to one hundred eighty zettabytes per year.[8] That means the amount of data we produce is doubling every two years and accelerating (see the chart on page 12). At that rate, within the next 200 years we will exceed the capacity available if we had the ability to store one bit of data on every atom in the solar system.

But we're getting ahead of ourselves. Before we explore the Bottomless Cloud, we need to understand why the electric utility analogy begins to break down when we apply it to the cloud. Although it may be an easy analogy to relate to, it's

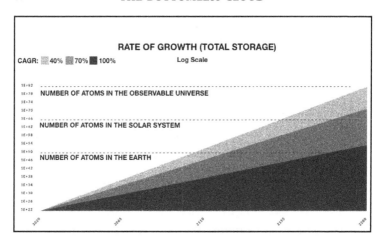

The different shaded wedges in the chart above, and their correspond-ing increasing data storage projections, reflect three rates of growth in data storage: 40%, 70%, and 100% CAGR. Even with the most conservative estimates we will exceed the capacity to store one bit on every atom that makes up the Earth by the year 2200.

also seriously flawed, as are the early cloud storage solutions that ushered it in. The reason is that, unlike electricity, data is *not* a commodity.

DATA IS NOT
A COMMODITY

Despite the common quip, data is not
the new oil. While every engine uses the
same basic sort of fuel, every business is
fueled by its own unique set of data.

In the case of electricity or any other utility, the product being delivered is a pure, undifferentiated commodity. Setting aside reliability and slight variances in cost, 120 volts and 100 amps of electric service is no different regardless of who your provider is. The same is true for natural gas, water, oil, gasoline, or any other utility.

But in the case of data, you're not dealing with an undifferentiated commodity. Data is increasingly the single most important differentiator in how companies innovate, serve their customers, and gain insight into their markets. It is the competitive battlefield of the future.

For instance, Uber's vast warehouse of transactional, behavioral, and geographic data is the foundation of its business and Uber's core differentiator. The same is true of Netflix, whose digital content and the data about the behaviors and preferences of viewers are the company's crown jewels.

In fact, we'd suggest that the same applies to every modern enterprise. The data is ultimately the most important competitive differentiator. However, if you pay close attention to how companies such as Uber and Netflix are using data, you'll see that their attitude is not one of minimizing the data footprint in order to decrease its volume, but rather to gather as much data as possible through as many interactions as possible. The assumption being that each piece of data increases in value with each new piece of data captured. And that brings us to the quote that we started this chapter with, Data is NOT the New Oil.

A quick search on Google will reveal dozens of articles that talk about data as the next big commodity, sometimes comparing it with oil. Maybe it's a provocative headline, but there is nothing the least bit commodity-like about data.

There's a brand-x gas station called "Sid's Gas." The big sign over the pumps reads "Sid says, 'Gas is gas. Why pay more?'" He's right. A gallon of his generic brand of gas gets you exactly the same number of miles as a gallon of Mobil or Shell gas. A barrel of oil purchased by a refinery is worth exactly the same as any other barrel of similar quality oil. Commodities are by definition interchangeable. Think oil, steel, broadband, or electricity, to name a few. With electricity, there are thousands of power companies. You can plug my phone charger into any outlet in the world and it works. That's what a commodity is.

Articles that have appeared recently on the subject explain that data is the "new oil" that powers the information economy. There's no doubt that data powers the information economy, but that doesn't make data a commodity any more than you would say that cars are a commodity, or fashion accessories, or beer are a commodity. They are not interchangeable or equivalent. In fact, it is the uniqueness of data that gives it value and drives the profits of the companies that use it. Data represents knowledge, and if you know the same things that

I know, you have no advantage over me. So, it's worth your while to invest in acquiring data that I don't have. It's the opposite of a commodity.

Here are a few examples:

Facebook acquires a lot of data about its users. It then uses that data to generate over $40 billion of advertising revenue. If Google and everybody had the same data, advertisers could beat up suppliers to get a much lower price. Facebook's data is in no way a commodity. Its uniqueness powers one of the world's most valuable and influential companies.

Retailers like CVS keep careful track of your purchases. They know what kind of shampoo you like and they even know exactly how much you use. This allows them to offer deals on shampoo at just the right time. The data they accumulate (and carefully guard) drives the business and personalizes the shopping experience in a way that someone without that data cannot.

So while storage is definitely a commodity, the data being stored—your data—is not a commodity. In almost every case, it will be unique to your organization. And your ability to discover uses for your data that helps you run your business better can give you a competitive edge. For example, Google Maps knows where more people are more than any other navigation app. Let's say that your town reverses the direction of a one-way street. Even without their informing Google of the change, people will start going down the street the "wrong" way, and the application will learn from the data that something has changed. If a competitor hasn't learned to do the same analysis on the data, or is too small to have enough data to discover the change, then Google is likely to come off as the better mapping app.

"Gas is gas" and "storage is storage." But data is not data. Your company's future rests on the fact that data is becoming increasingly valuable and proprietary, and therefore worth storing in the Cloud indefinitely.

So, if we stop thinking of data as a pure commodity and return to our earlier assumption that each piece of data increases in value with each new piece of data captured, we'll see, in the case of the Bottomless Cloud, that the value of data is amplified in countless ways as long as the economic benefit of data exceeds the cost of its storage.

The problem is that the solutions used by first generation providers of cloud storage were, and in many cases, still are stuck in an industrial era mindset of scarcity, in which data storage is seen as a cost of doing business that needs to be carefully managed and conserved. But applying the scarcity mindset to the technologies of data storage severely limits your ability to differentiate and innovate. According to a report by market analyst Tech Pro Research:[9]

"Despite the discussions about burgeoning data and the need to get strategic about storage, storage is still viewed in enterprises as a commodity asset. It therefore comes as no surprise that the major pain point for 68 percent of those [we] surveyed is cost of storage."

Consider the analogy of telecommunications. During the better part of the 20th century, companies diligently managed and restricted the use of telecommunications, which were still metered and whose access was tightly controlled. Companies closely monitored telecommunication usage to make sure phone usage was not abused.

In most organizations, phone usage was a privilege that was carefully allocated. International calls were restricted to only when necessary. Employees who "abused" the privilege were chastised and their use limited. You needed a code to "dial out." This is a scarcity model that emphasizes the minimization and prioritization of a service based on where existing operations of the business warrant its use.

With the advent of VOIP (Voice Over IP), services such as Skype, unlimited usage plans, and limitless bandwidth, all of this suddenly changed. Today telecommunications operates with a mindset of abundance. We do not think about the cost of each call. In fact, the opposite is true. We outright ignore the value vs cost equation. Nobody considers the explicit value

In the case of data, you're not dealing with an undifferentiated commodity. Data is increasingly the single most important differentiator in how companies innovate, serve their customers, and gain insight into their markets. It is the competitive battlefield of the future.

of a long-distance phone call before weighing it against its cost. After all, when is the last time you actually looked at your phone bill?

The attitude is that every connection has some value; however, we do not know which ones will have the greatest value, so we do not differentiate the important calls from the unimportant when it comes to determining which ones are worth the cost. And that's exactly what we mean by "Bottomless."

In addition, unlike any other utility, the value of data is not singular or absolute. Data that has no value today may be extraordinarily valuable in the future. The need to decide which data is important and which is not is an artifact of the past when storage space and square footage were synonymous.

The same collection of data can also be mined repeatedly in different ways to create new value. Take, for example, a media company that has millions of hours of analog film footage from movies and TV shows, which it has archived.

Occasionally a popular show may be digitized and sold to viewers or distributors. In a scarcity model, the process of selecting the shows to convert to digital form would be based on current demand, focus groups, broad social trends, and current events. The likely result would be that most of the company's profits (80%) would come from a relatively small number of assets, products, or services (20%).

That 80/20 rule, also called the Pareto principle after Italian economist Vilfredo Pareto, has been a staple of the 20th century and applies to nearly every industrial era scarcity model of doing business. But Pareto's principle only works when there is a higher incremental cost or additional friction associated with the other 80% of assets, products, or services. Friction is anything that adds to the time, cost, or resources needed to perform a business function, or which detracts from the customer experience.

In the physical world, engineers describe a machine that works at 100% efficiency as being frictionless, meaning that it runs in an idealized manner without the inherent burden of mechanical friction that slows its components. But friction is not just a concept that applies to mechanical devices.

Take, for example, an incandescent bulb in which only 20% of the energy used by even the most efficient bulb is converted to light. The rest simply dissipates as useless heat as compared to the new generation of LED bulbs where over 90% of the energy is converted to light.

That may not be the way we are accustomed to thinking of friction but it's a fundamental shift that is driving a new way of doing business.

In short, doing more with less.

It's no different in the case of the Cloud, which removes much of the friction of storing and managing data by making the infrastructure needed to handle data a commodity.

So, if we go back to our media company as an example, what if the company's entire film library were suddenly digitized so that there was no additional cost or friction associated with the ongoing access to any video? How much additional revenue might the company be able to recognize as a result?

Q Where is the data friction in your business and how are you reducing it?

If we use Amazon as an example, nearly 60% of Amazon's book sales come from the 80% of books that would otherwise not be available through traditional retailers. While these are not all digital or eBooks, the premise is that they would not be available to buyers were it not for Amazon's ability to datify the buying process and thereby make the incremental cost of selling even the most obscure books just as frictionless as selling popular books.

Until recently, most data storage strategies have used the fact that the vast majority of corporate revenues have come

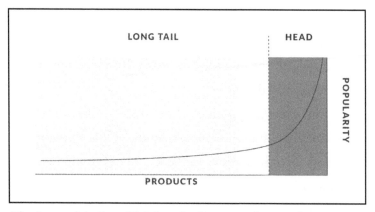

The theory of the Long Tail describes how our culture and economy are increasingly shifting away from a focus on a relatively small number of "hits" (mainstream products and markets) at the head of the demand curve and toward a huge number of niches in the tail. (Chris Anderson, www.thelongtail.com)

from a relatively small percentage of their data. This is the essence of an industrial age scarcity model. However, if a business can digitize the long tail of their data assets, it can significantly increase its topline revenues. For example, in the case of Amazon, each percentage of the long tail increases Amazon's overall book revenues by 0.75%.

This phenomenon of the "long tail" is a cornerstone of abundance thinking because we no longer have to obsess over which subset of data will hold the greatest value in the future, result in a new innovation, or new business opportunities.[10]

For our media company, that would mean it could more than double its revenues by making its assets digitally available. While this does not factor in the costs for an initial digital conversion and the smaller incremental costs for storage, even if these reduce payback by half, a company's bottom line can typically be increased by nearly 30% by tapping into otherwise archived data.

This isn't just a hypothetical discussion. Datafication is the competitive strategy that companies such as Amazon and Hulu have already used to outflank existing studios such as MGM and Paramount.

This simple shift in thinking, from scarcity to abundance, and from friction to friction-less, also creates opportunities for entirely new innovations and business models. For instance, our media company could now use customer viewing behaviors to suggest a hyperpersonalized viewing experience, which may only appeal to a market of a few hundred individuals (or, for that matter, just one individual), without having to justify the creation or the cost of a customized offering!

In fact, going back to electrification, the more interesting story of the utility model is not about electric power plants and the electric grid, but about what happened to the factories that used it once

Datafication is also not just a conceptual exercise. We can translate it directly to revenue growth and profitability.

they got out of the power generation business. As power utilities came online during the 1900s, factories for the first time in history, did not have to worry about generating and managing their own power. They were no longer tied to a single water wheel of innovation and could instead focus on the things that really mattered—the innovation of their products and services.

It's no coincidence that manufacturing experienced a surge of innovation in the early part of the 20th century. With the increasing ability to focus on their core processes and products, companies developed a far more sophisticated approach to manufacturing. The impact was felt across all industries, from moving assembly lines in automobile manufacturing to farming and agriculture.

Consider that in 1905, there were 50,000 individual power plants in the United States, most owned and managed by businesses whose core competency was not power generation. Today, there are approximately 2,300![11]

Yet the collective economic output (GDP) of the USA has increased from only 500 billion to just under 19 trillion. That's a nearly forty-fold increase, and with 0.5% of the electric utility providers!

The same may hold true for data storage. Today, nearly every enterprise has its own data storage capabilities. In most cases, the technology of storing data is no more relevant to the enterprise's core competency than power generation would be. If history repeats itself, 10 years from now, a relatively small number of cloud storage companies will be responsible for nearly all stored data, and on-premises data storage will largely become a thing of the past.

We're not claiming that all of this growth was due to the advent of electric utilities; there clearly was much more that spurred economic growth during that period. But few would argue that reliable power and the foundational concept of external economies of scale, which was at the heart of the electric utility model, played a significant role.

So, here's a question. If the utility model works so well, why is it that there are still many factories that generate their own electricity, accounting for a whopping 200 billion kilowatt hours, or 13 percent of all electricity consumed in manufacturing? And that percentage is increasing as alternative power options such as solar and wind continue to fall in cost.[12]

It's because the highly vertically integrated utility model is breaking down as we move past the industrial era.

The problem with the utility model, for both traditional utilities and with cloud utilities, such as those offered by Amazon, Google, and Microsoft, is two-fold: first they continue to use a scarcity mindset for both the technology architecture and the pricing of their services, an approach which severely stifles innovation; second, they bundle all aspects of the Cloud (storage, computing, platform) in one vertically integrated offering, where the customer does not have the choice to pick best of breed in each category.

As organizations struggle under the weight, costs, and

volatility of information and business systems that are relentlessly churning out data, they have increasingly been turning to these first-generation cloud vendors as a way to manage all of their information technology costs and risks, since that has been their only option. This was a captive business model, which lured businesses with the promise of lower costs, but which then locked them into a data fortress from which there was no way out. Until now.

A new breed of cloud storage is making its way onto the market as an alternative, one that was "Born in the Cloud." And it has the potential to change business models in ways that will likely make the disruption and the progress of electrification, and its impact on the industrial revolution, pale by comparison.

By the way, a short aside before we go on; with all this talk about the evolution of electric utilities you may be wondering how the current trend of installing solar panels on residential and commercial rooftops fits into our analogy of the move towards third-party utilities.

It's important to note that individuals and companies putting solar panels on their roofs, and calling that "going off the grid," are not necessarily doing that. In fact, the vast majority of solar panels are producing electricity that goes back into the grid.

While the ability to produce power locally points to a hybrid approach for how the utility of the future may operate, it's important to keep in mind that the reason this works with electricity is because it is a pure commodity. Electrons are electrons. Trading and exchanging electrons with competitors does not put you at a competitive disadvantage.

However, as we've said, data is not a commodity. So, investing in local storage still creates an economic liability since you are not going to sell back any excess storage capacity to other companies who may also be competitors.

The Cloud is infinitely scalable, meaning that it grows as your needs grow. This is often referred to as elasticity, meaning that you use the Cloud, and invest in it, based on the needs you have at any given moment, rather than being required to buy excess capacity and resources in anticipation of growth.

Aligning value and risk is one of the Cloud's greatest benefits. By scaling to actual success rather than trying to predict the success of your business, you significantly alter the relationship between risk and investment by capping your downside while leaving the upside unlimited.

This isn't limited to the digital world. Something very similar has already been done in manufacturing with Just In Time inventory management. In order to align value and risk, manufacturers developed sophisticated supply chain systems that projected production requirements so that parts were shipped precisely when needed.

So, rather than keep large inventories on hand, only what

was absolutely necessary was delivered to the factory. This can be an enormous competitive advantage. For example, one of the reasons that Apple is considered a global leader in supply chain is that it turns over its inventory in less than five days, whereas a competitor such as Samsung takes up to two weeks.

Just In Time principles are also applicable to cloud data storage. Having data in the Cloud instantly available is critical. Otherwise your processes are constantly waiting on the delivery of data. The effect is similar to having to stop the assembly line while you wait on the delivery of essential parts! One point, or analog, worth considering is that Just In Time manufacturing reduces inventory. Inventory carries significant hidden costs. There are the obvious ones, like the cost of financing the value of the inventory, but then there are also the costs of storing it, counting it for audits, the logistical systems needed to retrieve inventory, the well-documented relationship between the quantity of inventory and "inventory shrinkage" (meaning theft or simply misplacement) and ultimately write-downs or scrapping of obsolete inventory.

When it comes to data storage, excess capacity represents excess inventory. It is estimated that on-premises data storage typically utilizes only 60-70% of available capacity. Often this loading factor is not taken into account when comparing the cost of on-premises storage to cloud storage where inventory is generally zero. Another factor that is frequently overlooked in calculating the cost of storage is periodic replacement of hardware. For example, manufacturers of LTO (Linear Tape-Open) tapes tout their extremely low cost. However, that calculation is usually based on the premise that you can fill the tape up 100% and store it offline, presumably in a cardboard box in a warehouse somewhere, for up to 20 years.

The fallacy with this calculation is that 20 years from now you may not be able to read the tape because the tape drives will have long since become obsolete and scrapped and the tapes themselves may be unreadable due to an accumulation of random bit errors. Furthermore, a tape that is stored in a salt mine in Utah, for example, is so difficult, expensive, and time-consuming to retrieve, that the cost of the data retrieval may render the data useless. In fact, our estimates show that 98% of the data stored this way is never retrieved. That doesn't mean that 98% of data has no value it simply means that the cost of retrieving exceeds the value of the data. With the Bottomless Cloud that 98% is going to be just as inexpensive to retrieve and to access as the other 2%. That's the essence of the Bottomless Cloud.

Q **How does your cloud storage strategy align risk and value for unlimited upside?**

THE EVOLUTION OF THE CLOUD

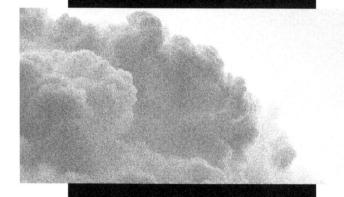

With Cloud 1.0, data was built around the business. With a Bottomless Cloud, the business is built around the data.

The Cloud represents the consummate disruptor to structure and traditional business models. It's a pervasive social and economic network that will soon connect and define more of the world than any other political, social, or economic organization, yet we are still looking at it primarily as a way to cut costs. Reducing data storage costs is only the first wave of a cloud-based storage architecture; it's the fundamental value proposition of Cloud 2.0. However, as we move into the next generation of storage solutions, Cloud 2.0, and the Bottomless Cloud, other, more valuable, benefits begin to emerge.

> Reducing data storage costs is only the first wave of a cloud-based storage architecture.

The Pre-Cloud On-Premises Solution

Even before cloud storage was an option, companies developed storage strategies to optimize data access and costs. Much of this was done by creating a data storage architecture that prioritized data based on its usefulness into online, nearline, offline, archival, and destroyed.

Transactional data that needed to be close at hand, and which was used on a frequent basis, was stored online in an organization's internal network so that it could be easily managed, accessed, and updated. Less frequently used data may have been stored on devices that were not constantly online but which could still be accessed with relative ease, what we called nearline data. Data that had outlived its useful life or was rarely accessed was offline or archived, usually off-site where both the media it was stored on and the real estate it was stored in were far less expensive. And data was no longer considered more valuable than the cost to store it was destroyed.

The reason for this was primarily cost-based. However, it was also the case that less data online meant that fewer devices were needed to store it. That all made perfect sense in an era of data scarcity which focused on conserving resources based on how well they supported the current business model.

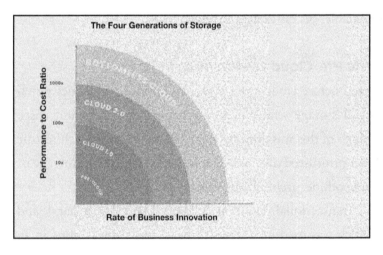

As cloud storage solutions have progressed through each successive generation of technology, performance has increased, costs have dropped, and most importantly, the rate of business model innovation has increased, ultimately spurring the creation of new industries.

However, that started to change 10 years ago as large technology companies began offering the option of cloud-based storage and computing, which promised to lower storage costs and eliminate the need for companies to manage their data. That first generation is what we're calling Cloud 1.0.

Cloud 1.0 Storage as a Utility

Cloud 1.0 is the utility model of cloud computing which relies on the benefits of building economies of scale where resources are shared across a large network of customers. As with electricity to your home, you pay as you use it. The utility deals with the issues of peak load, infrastructure, and delivery. You just worry about turning the switch on.

> Datafication is the wholescale transformation of the business model by rebuilding the business around the data.

This simple proposition had huge value for many companies, but it was especially advantageous for smaller and midsize businesses that couldn't play the "what if" game when it came to guessing how much storage they would need. It's also a far more secure model for these businesses, half of which don't even bother to backup their data.

When cloud storage providers talk about "elastic storage," it is this cost-cutting aspect of the cloud that they are most often addressing. The fundamental value proposition of Cloud 1.0 was that it was supposed to be less expensive because you only purchased and used what you needed.

While Cloud 1.0 is only the first generation of true cloud-based storage, it has experienced rapid growth and become the goose that laid the golden egg for large players like Amazon whose 2017 operating income was almost entirely (89%) due to AWS (its full suite of cloud services).[13]

Although Cloud 1.0 does not change the way data is used, the lower cost of storage and the ability to offload the burden of managing a physical storage infrastructure has accelerated the move towards business models that are driven by data.

For Netflix, Data Is the Business

Netflix is perhaps one of the best examples of the transition between Cloud 1.0 and Cloud 2.0 through its use of behavioral data in creating new products and services. By analyzing the individual viewing habits of its one hundred million members, the company is able to understand behaviors at an unprecedented level of detail. As Joris Evers, Netflix's former Director of Global Communications, once quipped, "There are 33 million different versions of Netflix."

Not only does Netflix use individualized behavioral data to make recommendations to members, but it also uses this data to produce its own original content. For example, when Netflix dished out one hundred million dollars to purchase the rights to produce *House of Cards*, it was betting on a trove of data

Q Are you building your business model around your data, or are you force-fitting your data to an old business model?

which, among other things, indicated that director David Fincher and the British version of *House of Cards* formed a sort of perfect storm for the interests of its members (at least it was at the time).[14]

Netflix goes to what might appear to be absurd lengths to understand and cater to its members at a very fine degree of resolution. It has 76,897 microgenres of movies. When it develops the identity for a new movie, it will analyze the specific color content of promotional images for other successful movies and series. It even has a 36-page manual that is used to train specialized movie "viewers," who are tasked with watching movies and using metatagging to indicate everything from how sexually explicit or violent a movie is to the moral character of the actors.[15]

When you view a trailer for a new Netflix movie or series, you will see one that is optimized for your behavioral style.

While Netflix may appear to be strictly in the business of creating and delivering content, its real competitive advantage, and the reason it is such a threat to traditional studios, is the way it has built its business around the data.

While Cloud 1.0 provided a way to transition storage to the cloud, both the technology it was built on and the pricing models early providers of Cloud 1.0 used were nearly identical to what was used for on-premises storage solutions. Although Cloud 1.0 was just marginally cheaper in some cases, more often it was more expensive due to access and egress fees (costs to retrieve and move data). That's not to say that these solutions were not revolutionary at the time. Amazon's vision behind AWS (Amazon Web Service) and IaaS (Infrastructure as a Service) broke new ground by setting out to create nothing less ambitious than an operating system for the Internet.

However, in many ways, cloud storage was an afterthought for early Cloud 1.0 vendors, whose primary objective was not the creation of a cloud storage capability, but

The problem with the utility model, for both traditional utilities and with cloud utilities, such as those offered so far by Amazon and Microsoft, is that they continue to use a scarcity mindset for both the technology architecture and the pricing of their services, an approach which severely stifles innovation.

rather a cloud-based computing capability. Simply put, cloud computing was the ability to move computer processing power, software applications, and the various platform components of computing (networks, operating systems) from an on-premises to an off-premises solution.

In order to provide vertically integrated solutions, Amazon, Microsoft, Google, and other providers of Cloud 1.0 included storage as a necessary, albeit secondary, consideration. That wasn't an issue when there were no other options for cloud storage. However, integrated Cloud 1.0 storage solutions have become captive platforms that are next to impossible to walk away from once a business adopts them as its cloud storage vendor of choice.

Amazon's vision seems to be "Your whole data center in our cloud." The strategy is to provide all the capabilities of a data center, from storage, to computing, to content distribution, to analytics, etc., in a single solution. While there is an appeal to that, it does not provide for best of breed or lowest cost for each component of the Cloud.

For example, egress fees make it difficult for people to compare the cost of moving to the Cloud vs maintaining an on-premises infrastructure. With on-premises data storage, most people have no idea how much "egress" they use. They would have trouble even metering such a statistic if they wanted to. Consequently, migrating to the Cloud carries the risk that costs are unknowable in advance.

Unlocking the Power of Data

The result of these convoluted costs models was that as businesses moved their data into Cloud 1.0, it didn't take them long to realize that they had a Gordian knot of immense proportions to deal with in determining even the cost of their cloud storage.

In the case of Amazon, for example, customers had to identify which collections of data were not as critical to have immediately accessible and to then store these on lower cost storage (in Amazon's case, a product aptly named Glacier). They then had to pick from three tiers of availability on Glacier: Expedited, Standard, and Bulk.

As a result, an entire cottage industry sprang into existence just to help businesses moving to Cloud 1.0 understand and calculate pricing!

This sort of approach is eerily similar to the evolution of telecommunications, which we talked about earlier. There was a time when you would have hired a telecom pricing specialist to decipher your phone bill, usage trends, and then suggest ways to reconfigure providers in order to optimize your telecom spending. So confident were these consultants of the bloat in your phone bill that they typically billed for their services as a percentage of what was saved.

In that same light, Cloud 1.0 providers were creating unnecessary complexity by using the storage rules of the past, which relied on complex tiered architectures and the minimization of online data.

As is always the case in a free market, an increase in complexity creates an opportunity for simplification and innovation. At the heart of this was the transition from

Cloud 1.0 which used a scarcity mindset to build external economies of scale, to the next generation of storage, Cloud 2.0, which used an abundance mindset to build economies of scope.

Economies of Scale Versus Economies of Scope

An economy of scale is a well-understood model that is at the heart of the industrial era. As industries grow, they inevitably take on the burden of creating new services, machines, and methods for supporting their growth, whether it be running the in-house cafeteria to feed a growing staff, a shuttle bus to transport workers, the power to run their factory, or the devices to store their data.

However, companies that do this are creating distractions from their core competency, increasing risk (since these services are not what they do best), and ultimately innovating these services very little since they are not likely to invest in R&D for something that is ancillary to their business. As we saw with our example of electrification, at some point the consolidation of these functions across the business makes sense since it reduces the cost of the service and increases the rate of innovation, by handing it over to someone for whom it is a core competency.

That has been and will continue to be the case across all industries. Economies of scale are not going away. But what has been simultaneously evolving are companies that focus on economies of scope.

Economies of scope create a digital ecosystem in which companies can easily connect to and expand into adjacent markets and new business models. Companies that compete based on economies of scope are obsessively data-centric. One of the best examples is Nike, which has transformed itself from a provider of sneakers and clothing into a lifestyle and fitness company that is intimately linked to technology and healthcare vendors.

Q How do you use data to redefine your brand and become the next Under Armour?

In 2015, Nike CEO Mark Parker described this in a call with investors where he talked about how Nike is partnering with the NBA, "I've talked with commissioner Adam Silver about our role enriching the fan experience. What can we do to digitally connect the fan to the action they see on the court? How can we learn more about the athlete, real-time?"[16]

Another example, and fierce competitor of Nike's, is Under Armour. According to its CEO Kevin Plank, "Brands that do not evolve and offer the consumer something more than a product will be hard-pressed to compete in 2015 and beyond."[17]

Nike and Under Armour may not be the first companies you think of when data comes to mind; however, their basis for competition and their ability to connect with the customer stem directly from their ability to capture as much data as possible about their customers through technologies such as wearables and embedded sensor.

Cloud 2.0 Born in the Cloud

While Cloud 1.0 storage provided the promise of lower storage costs, it was still based on the industrial era scarcity mindset that we've described as obsessed with limiting the amount of data stored. And that model would not have supported a new data-driven business for either Nike or Under Armour.

This approach is often referred to as a "lift and shift" solution that simply replaced on-premises storage with off-site storage, which cost marginally less due to the economies of scale for third-party providers. It made perfect sense at the time, given how data had been used and how much it cost to store. However, not only was technology changing, but the way in which data was being used was also changing.

New companies such as Uber and Netflix began to digitally disrupt industrial era business models by building data-centered business through what we call datafication.

Datafication is the natural successor to digitization. Digitization is the conversion of analog data to digital form and it has been the primary contributor to new growth in storage capacity for the past 60 years. Digitization made existing processes faster and easier to scale by removing the friction of paper-based communications and transactions. It clearly had an impact on the innovation of a business's existing transactional systems, but it didn't do much to change the underlying business model.

It's critical to emphasize this last point. Talk about digital transformation has been rampant. However, any successful digital transformation initiative has to be based on a foundation of datafication. If the data that represents the business, its customers, and suppliers is not adequately captured, managed, and accessible, digital transformation ends up being nothing but incremental change to the business, since it is still using the same old scarcity-driven data model.

Datafication, however, is the wholescale transformation of the business model by rebuilding the business around the data. And this is not only transactional data and documents, but the much larger treasure trove of behavioral data that is suddenly available through the evolution and proliferation of internet-connected devices and sensors.

In addition, storage technology was changing. Newer storage devices and software offered faster retrieval times, greater reliability and fewer mechanical problems, as well as significantly lower overall costs. This led to the evolution of Cloud 2.0 solutions that were not just repurposing premises-based storage for the Cloud but also developing solutions that were specifically Born in the Cloud and which could now take advantage of a business model that refocused on data abundance. By the way, Cloud 2.0 still relies heavily

Against this deluge of data, Cloud 1.0 stands little chance of being the predominant approach for progressive organizations that expect to build sustainable and scalable cloud storage strategies. on the benefits of cost savings when moving to the Cloud. In some cases, these are one fifth of the cost of Cloud 1.0 solutions; however, it also brings new technologies and a new mindset to the Cloud.

Datafication rests on the basic premise that restricting data use is only partially useful in very specific situations where data needs to be destroyed due to regulatory or legal constraints. In all other cases, the objective is to adopt a mindset of abundance and keep as much data as possible available for as long as possible. It's what some Cloud 2.0 providers call "Hot Storage," implying that all data is equally accessible and potentially valuable.

Contrast this with Amazon's approach, which uses storage tiers that are much like different grades of gasoline. Lower cost tiers like Glacier are deliberately hobbled to protect the higher profit margins on the fastest product, S3. Just as it wouldn't make much sense to have three different electrical outlets in your wall for good, flaky, and completely unreliable electricity, it's much simpler and less expensive overall to have only one tier of storage. If Cloud 2.0 storage is faster than S3 and cheaper than Glacier, why would you want to have different tiers and all the complexity associated with trying to determine what data should go in what tier?

This is bound to strike initial chords of fear in most people who are accustomed to archiving and destroying data. But the value of data typically far exceeds the resources of most organizations to store it given its historical costs for on-premises or Cloud 1.0 solutions.

Take, for example, the use of body cams and surveillance video, both of which have become indispensable allies to law enforcement. Body cam footage is destroyed on average 75 days after it is taken, although the statute of limitations for prosecuting a crime averages seven years. That severely minimizes the value of body cams as an effective law enforcement tool as well as a means of protecting citizens' rights.

For example, a widely publicized story about nurse Alex Wubbels, who was involved in an emergency room altercation with police, made it into major news media broadcasts on September 1st, 2017. However, the event happened on July 26th. In many states, that footage would have been destroyed within 30- 60 days due to the cost of keeping it, even as an archive.

In the case of body cams, the only reason data isn't kept is cost. If the cost of data storage were zero, everyone would keep everything forever. We'll never get to that point, but we're certainly moving in that direction. If the cost of storage exceeds the value realized by storing the data, then throw it away. But if the cost drops to the point where the value exceeds the cost, then keep it. With the typical 80% cost savings of a Cloud 2.0 solution the economics of what to keep change dramatically.

Everyone in the IT industry has to deal with this tradeoff almost daily. You can likely recall when your IT department used to get tied in knots if your email exceeded 100MBs. Today most people can search email going back years without worrying about the cost. This same principle applies to virtually all data storage. You can see your bank statements going back almost 10 years. It used to be 3 months. What drives these decisions is the value of having the data accessible vs. the cost of storing it.

Despite this, many companies that have bought into Cloud 1.0 find it nearly impossible to make the migration to Cloud 2.0. That's often the plight of early technology adopters who rush to a new solution as it is still evolving. We're not being overly critical of these early adopters since the lure is understandable. However, for companies that have not yet moved to the Cloud, they would be well advised to skip Cloud 1.0 and go directly to Cloud 2.0.

Even for organizations that have until now resisted moving to a Cloud solution, what will make the need for Cloud 2.0 abundantly clear is the increasing volume of data that will be needed to fuel technologies such as Artificial Intelligence and new business models that are just starting to emerge. (See the next chapter, "Where Tomorrow's Data Will Come From.")

The volumes of data involved in these new applications and businesses will be staggering, stretching our imagination well beyond any prior precedent. Against this deluge of data, Cloud 1.0 stands little chance of being the solution for progressive organizations that expect to build sustainable and scalable cloud storage strategies.

The Bottomless Cloud

As we've already discussed, cloud storage is not just about technology; it is about how your business is run. As the ability to store data economically, and to access it quickly, changes so do the potential business models of organizations or those of an entire industry.

For instance, consider our earlier example of media and entertainment, where the overwhelming majority of film and video assets are still in analog form. Being able to digitize those assets and to then combine them with the datafication of consumer behaviors creates entirely new ways to deliver media hyperpersonalized to consumers' experiences.

These new business models are also far more collaborative

> The majority of tomorrow's data will be external.
> It will be data about behaviors, data generated by autonomous devices, and data collected from vast networks of sensors.

since they allow the development of digital ecosystems within which companies can easily share, combine, and repurpose digital assets across extensive partner networks. Not only does this benefit larger organizations with many partners, but it also creates enormous opportunity for smaller businesses, which can now create large virtualized networks of digital ecosystem partners.

Most importantly, a Bottomless Cloud strategy allows you to think differently about the very role of data, data centers, and the Cloud. A Bottomless Cloud removes the constraints that otherwise restrict the ability to innovate new business models, products, and services that extend well beyond the data boundaries of the past—stretching both our organizations and our imaginations.

However, the challenge in adopting a Bottomless Cloud strategy is not technology or cost, since these are quickly evolving, but instead, the change in mindset from conserving, archiving, and destroying data, to mining and exploiting it in abundance.

One of the best examples of this is that of autonomous vehicles (AVs). One of the least often talked about implications of AVs is that their relationship with the Cloud is radically different than almost any device in the past. (By the way, what we're about to describe applies equally to any device that relies on AI and even rudimentary machine learning.)

The decisions an AV makes consist of two critical

The yearly storage requirements for an AV using Cloud 1.0 would be nearly ten times the cost of the automobile!

components; first, they need to be made fast, typically in fractions of a second, and second, the AV needs to learn from its decisions as well as the decisions of other AVs. The implications of this are fascinating and unexpected. Due to the speed with which decisions need to be made, the AV requires significant onboard computing power and data storage capability. The increase in onboard data storage is the result of all of the sensors, contextual data about the vehicle and its environment, and data gathered from communication with other AVs in its proximity. This onboard data is used for real-time decision-making, since the latency of communicating with the Cloud can be a severe impediment to the speed with which these decisions need to be made.

However, the volumes of data that go into the real-time decision making then need to be uploaded to the Cloud to fuel the learning which is so critical to future decisions. This creates a cycle of decision-making and learning that dramatically accelerates the rate of both data capture and storage.

The net effect is that while an AV today may generate somewhere in the neighborhood of one to twenty TB of data per hour,[18] the increase on onboard sensors from a few dozen to hundreds, as AVs progress to full autonomy, will result in a commensurate increase of data storage requirements, with the potential for a single AV to generate several hundred terabytes hourly. Storing this all onboard is well outside of the scope of any technology available today or in the foreseeable future. Yet it is also well outside of the cost-effective scope of Cloud 1.0 storage.

For example, the yearly storage requirements for an AV with typical Cloud 1.0 storage options would be over half a million dollars; nearly ten times the cost of the automobile!

The bottom line is that AI feeds on data, and lots of data. While we've used AVs as an example, listing all of the potential uses are impossible since many of them do not yet exist.

For example in astronomy, many of the most significant discoveries of comets, exo-planets, and meteors were discovered with new AI algorithms grinding their way through mountains of old observations. In biotech, cancer cures have been discovered by algorithms that find genetic similarities among large populations. In physics, particle colliders take millions of pictures per second. Years later, new AI algorithms comb through massive amounts of data to discover new particles and answer fundamental questions about particle physics.

While we cannot project all of the ways a Bottomless Cloud will alter today's enterprises, there are some areas where we are already seeing enormous change and new business models emerging.

WHERE TOMORROW'S DATA WILL COME FROM

By 2100, there will be 100 times as many computing devices as there are grains of sand on all of the world's beaches, and every one of those devices will be churning out data.

The overwhelming majority of data stored today is internal transactional data related directly to the ongoing operations of the business. The good thing about internal data is that you can project and predict with relative accuracy the requirements for data storage and access since it's based on transaction volume.

AI is only as intelligent as the volume of data it has to learn from.

The majority of tomorrow's data will be external. It will be data about behaviors, data generated by autonomous devices, and data collected from vast networks of sensors. The data will be orders of magnitude greater in volume than the data we already collect.

While there are likely to be myriad sources of data that we cannot yet anticipate, many sources of external data are already starting to have an impact on how we think about the future demands on storage.

Artificial Intelligence

Most conversations about AI tend to focus on improvements in algorithms that can mimic intelligence. What's often missed in those conversations is that AI is only as intelligent as the volume of data it has to learn from. The recent advances in AI could simply not have been possible without our significantly increased ability to capture and store data. Google alone processes over 3.5 billion searches every day. That's more than one trillion searches yearly.

Google DeepMind's AlphaGo Zero, which won against both the world's human Go champion as well as against its predecessor AlphaGo, had to play 20 million games against itself to train its AI.

Of all the factors driving increases in data storage, none will be as pervasive as AI. The value of AI in countless applications and the cost savings it will deliver will drive adoption. Research by Deloitte projects labor savings due to AI in federal, state, and local government of over $40 billion.[19] If we apply the same savings to private industry, savings could exceed five trillion dollars annually. As extraordinary as that may seem, it is still calculating the value of AI using the scarcity economic models of the industrial era.

Rather than focus on cost savings alone, we also need to factor in the added value in new businesses, products, and services. Estimating this with precision is far more difficult; however, during the last 140 years of the industrial era, every reduction in the labor force brought about by technology savings has created far more jobs, economic opportunity, and new businesses than it has destroyed.[20] AI will amplify this effect many times over any prior technology. As we better understand AI's value, a virtuous cycle will begin to accelerate demand for data well beyond the anticipated rates of growth.

Autonomous Devices

Today's driverless vehicles use AI in a very narrow sense. In many ways their progress is being inhibited by the lack of enough data. This leads to one of the most pressing issues in the field of driverless vehicles and autonomous devices (what we are collectively calling AVs). In order to conserve storage, most of the algorithms that operate AVs are trained to gather specific data about a subset of the AV's context. However, the ideal way in which to train an AV is to allow it to learn the same way that human drivers do, by capturing all available data about context. This has a dramatic impact on the amount of data that needs to be stored, increasing data storage per hour from 500 GB an hour to 5 TB an hour.

> Labor savings due to AI in government are projected to be over $40 billion. In private industry, savings could exceed five trillion dollars annually.

Medicine

It's been estimated that up to 30% of all the data currently generated is for healthcare.[21] Research by McKinsey puts the potential healthcare value of using this data in new ways at $300 billion.[22] Clearly, that is not what's being done today. The overwhelming majority of that data is transient, archived, or simply not available in a time frame commensurate with the need. Hospitals and clinics are notorious for being unable to share patient data amongst themselves unless they are all on the same internal network. Even then, it can be a challenge. Half of all hospitals don't even have a basic Electronic Health Record.

Despite this poor state of affairs, new data continues to flood the current healthcare system. This is not only the case for increased precision of diagnostics and imaging, but also in new areas where medicine is making some of the greatest leaps forward.

For example, the ability to sequence the human genome, and to then personalize medicine to the individual, is being touted as one of the most important advances ever made in medicine, since it provides the ability to determine the individualized impact of pharmaceuticals and therapies to each individual.

DECREASE IN COST PER GENOME SEQUENCED 2001 - 2016

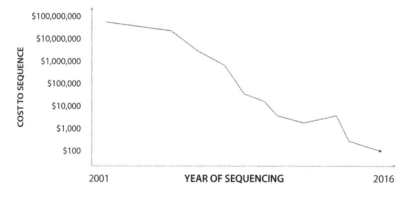

The cost of sequencing the human genome has fallen dramatically since the first genome was sequenced in 2001. The drop-in cost is actually three times that of the similar drop in storage costs as has been projected by Moore's law.

Much of this is being driven by the amazing decrease in the cost of sequencing the human genome, which has dropped from three hundred million dollars in 2000 (the cost of the original genome sequenced) to under ten million dollars in 2007, to one million dollars in 2008, to under one thousand dollars today. The expectation is that the cost will have dropped to under one hundred dollars within the next five years. This rate of decrease in the cost exceeds even that which is predicted by Moore's law when projecting the advance of semi-conductor technology. Add to this the promise of gene splicing and editing through technologies such as CRISPR (Clustered Regularly Interspaced Short Palindromic Repeats) and the data that is potentially involved starts to boggle the mind.

A single strand of DNA can store upwards of 700 TB of data.[23] In only 4 grams, we could store all of the world's data today. A single human has about 60 grams of DNA!

Digital Self/Digital Twin

In my book *Revealing The Invisible*, I describe the advent of the digital self and the digital twin as the "collection of data that intimately describes a person or an object in a way that makes it possible to predict future behaviors."

The amounts of data involved in the creation of these digital twins is staggering. Imagine that every person and object will have a digital counterpart that contains the entire history of behaviors throughout his, her, or its lifecycle.

… as much as 100 zettabytes (roughly 100 times as much storage as exists in total today) will be required just for the industrial data created by digital twins by 2025.

For example, in the case of an Airbus A350, each wing alone has 10,000 sensors.[24] In total, a typical A350 in service will generate up to ten terabytes of data each day. The GE or Rolls Royce engines alone, of even less sophisticated aircraft today, produce 500 GB of data every hour. And, at the high end of estimates, Cisco projects that 40TB an hour are produced by a Boeing 787.[25]

If you're like most people who first read these numbers, your reaction is to think, "That's ridiculous, what could you possibly do with all of that data? Don't you really only need a few vital readings to operate and maintain an airplane?" The answer is that it depends on the cost and the value of the data

Every person, place, object, and thing will soon have a digital self or digital twin; a digital representation that intimately describes a person or an object in a way that makes it possible to model current behaviors and to predict future behaviors. This means that we will be able to model in digital form the myriad otherwise invisible relationships, behaviors, and connections between these digital selves.

compared with the cost and value of the plane's operation and maintenance.

If the net value of capturing and storing the data is greater than the value it creates, the answer would be you don't need that much data. However, according to global management consultants Oliver Wyman, the net savings to aviation maintenance costs of having this data could be $5-$6 billion annually. To put that in perspective, it would increase the bottom line of the aviation industry by about 15%.

The benefit of this data is that it allows predictive analytics on each part of the plane in real time, allowing manufacturers to do preventative maintenance and to study aircraft and engine behavior in ways that traditional simulation could never have come close to.

However, digital twins will not be limited just to aviation. Every machine and nearly every object will have a similar collection of data. The volume of data created by these digital twins will eclipse anything we've experienced to date. Our projections show that as much as 100 zettabytes (roughly 100 times as much storage as exists in total today) will be required just for the industrial data created by digital twins by 2025.

Hyperpersonalization

Hyperpersonalization is the ability to understand the digital behaviors not only of ourselves but also of the devices, objects, and institutions with which we interact. Each of these can have a digital self or digital twin (the collection of its digitized behaviors) that interacts with other digital objects. The complex patterns of interactions among these objects may appear invisible or obscure to us, and radically different than the biases we have of how the visible world operates, but algorithms and AI can easily understand the patterns they form and then predict future behaviors.

The greatest value of innovation for the next one hundred years will come from understanding and revealing these invisible behaviors. For instance, on a typical day your behavior is captured by no less than 255 sensors in your home, office, roadways, and stores. This doesn't include the many sensors that are capturing your online behaviors in social media, web browsing, and email.

IoT

In each decade, starting with 1960, the total number of user computing devices has increased on average by one order of magnitude. Basically, you can just add a zero to the total number of devices each decade over the past seven decades. (Note from the chart on page 64 that some decades have had slower growth than this while others have had faster growth.)

If we assume that a computer such as a mainframe or minicomputer that can support x users is the equivalent of x devices, while a PC, laptop, tablet, or smartphone is a single device, then the total global number of computing devices translates into one thousand devices in 1960, one million in 1980, one billion in 2000, 10 billion in 2020, and 100 billion in 2030.

By the way, the trend shown in the Growth in Computing chart on the next page does not include billions of sensors, from fingerprint sensors to accelerometers, or the twenty-five billion microcontrollers—chips used in thousands of applications, from automotive to medicine—that were shipped in 2017 alone.

The solid top line on the Growth in Computing chart looks like a pretty steep curve already. If it continues on that trajectory we will end up with a nearly impossible-to-comprehend figure of 1,000,000,000,000,000,000,000 (10e21) devices by 2100.[26]

Let's put that into perspective. There are estimated to be 7.5x10e18 grains of sand on all the beaches in the world—that's less than 1 percent of the devices we're projecting by 2100.

Again, we realize the tendency to consider this absurd. However, consider how much more absurd it would have been if, in 1960, with at most a few thousand end user computing devices, someone had told you that by 2020 there would be over 10 billion, and, of those, three billion would easily fit into our pockets and purses.

The link between the growth in computing and data is inextricable. In fact, while computing devices grow at about one order of magnitude each decade, total data storage grows at a much faster rate of one order of magnitude every six years!

The inescapable trajectory of data is something that we cannot slow. Trying to turn this tide is the equivalent of staring down a tsunami.

No amount of wishful thinking is going to save you. Your options are to retreat and head for high ground, where you'll have lots of company, or learn to surf it.

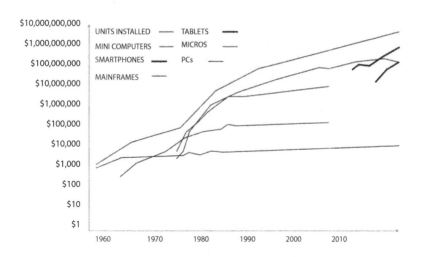

GROWTH IN COMPUTING (LOGARITHMIC SCALE)

The total "Units Installed" line for all computing devices (top solid line), including mainframes, minicomputers, microcomputers, PCs, smartphones, and tablets, shows how the number of devices has increased by roughly one order of magnitude each decade, even though individual technologies may have tapered off (e.g., mainframes, PCs) or been eliminated completely (e.g., mini and micro-computers).[27]

Movies / Video / Images

One of the most visible industries (apologies for the pun) where data has a direct impact on an organization's ability to monetize its digital assets is movies and entertainment.

According to IMDb there are:

- 3,054,974 TV episodes
- 589,086 Shorts
- 467,523 Movies
- 186,247 Videos
- 138,056 TV Series
- 120,905 TV Movies

That's a total of about 4,500,000 assets. Generously speaking, 50,000-100,000 of these (from 1%-2%) have been digitized. The rest are still stored in archival analog form (film). Guessing at the value of the archived footage is difficult. However, digitizing the movies alone would result in about 1,000,000 hours, which at 4K resolution, would create 318 petabytes of data (318 GB/hour). At today's Cloud 2.0 costs that would come to about $20M yearly in storage costs.

By the way, this is not a linear progression in storage requirement. It's exponential. As video resolution has gone from HD to 4K and now to 8K, the amount of data captured per second has gone up 4x and then 16x.

That means that if the long tail of the 4.5M in digital assets (98-99% of all assets) generated the same additional revenues as Amazon's long tail (.75% of revenue for each percent of the long tail) the TV and movie industry's revenues would increase by 73.5%.

It's worth noting here that we're only looking at historical assets not new ones being created. The rate at which video footage has been produced pales in comparison to the thousands of independent studios and hobbyists who are now arguably able to distribute video just as well as any major studio.

But the question that you're likely asking is, "How in the world will you ever be able to navigate millions and millions of hours of online video content?" The answer is that you won't! AI will do it for you. And this is where the notion of abundance, that we've been describing, steps in to once again radically alter our notion of what it means to capture and store data.

It's also worth noting here that more and more digital media assets are being stored in raw formats that consume far more data than compressed formats. The advantage of storing data in raw formats is that you don't have to wait for compression, you don't have to pay for the computers to do compression, and you don't lose any quality at all.

Take the simple analogy of your smartphone. According to Statstica, there were over 1.2 trillion photos taken with smartphones in 2017. While that averages to about 400 photos per smartphone user, our research shows that 10% of smartphone users have over 5,000 photos individually on their phones! There is simply no way to organize all of those photos without the assistance of AI.

In the same way, you will rarely concern yourself with navigation of entertainment assets. The keys to the kingdom in entertainment will go to whichever media provider best marshals the personalization of their digital assets to suit your individualized viewing needs and habits.

Companies that turn a blind eye to this are likely in the same frame of mind as Blockbuster whose execs, in response to an earnings call on which Netflix founder Reed Hastings derided Blockbuster by saying, "They've thrown everything at us but the kitchen sink!" did in fact overnight a stainless steel kitchen sink to Hastings. That's what happens when you're arrogance acts like a rearview mirror rather than a lens into the future.

Not to be too contrite about it, but entertainment companies ignoring the datafication of their industry will also go down the same drain.

Conclusion: Data Driven

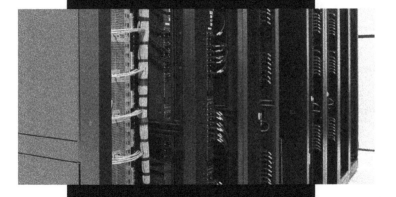

In an era of abundance, the value of data is in how much of it you can capture and mine; the greater the volumes, the greater the potential value.

Your business is data; it defines your market, it's your competitive advantage, it drives your innovation, profitability, and customer experience. In short, data is the single most important differentiator that will determine your organization's ability to survive and thrive.

Limiting the data captured and then throwing away as much of it as possible was necessary in an era of scarcity in which data was seen as an undifferentiated commodity that took up space and reduced the bottom line. It was the digital oil that fueled commerce and we used the bare minimum needed to efficiently run our businesses. Any excess was considered hazardous waste to be dumped as soon as possible.

However, as the volume of data has rapidly increased, savvy businesses have come to realize that there is opportunity hidden in the immense volumes of data; opportunity that is being amplified by new technologies, such as artificial intelligence, machine learning, data science and analytics, which allow us to gain unprecedented insight into the behaviors of markets, consumers, and organizations.

Our businesses are no longer constrained by the physical limitations of data storage and access, location, or bandwidth. As a result, new business models are emerging that rely on nearly unlimited storage to spur innovation and uncover new opportunity.

In an era of abundance, the value of data is in how much of it you can capture and mine; the greater the volumes, the greater the potential value. But realizing that value requires a new generation of cloud technologies, new business models, and new attitudes about data storage, which view data as the most critical asset of every business.

In this new framework, data is not the by-product of business; instead, the business is built around the data. Rather than constrain the business model, data continuously shapes and re-shapes it to meet the demands of fast moving and rapidly evolving markets.

New business models are emerging that rely on nearly unlimited storage to spur innovation and uncover opportunity.

Still, we have no doubt that many businesses will continue to invest in Cloud 1.0. In some cases that will be a brand-driven decision; in other cases, the appeal of a single vendor solution will play a role. For organizations not focused on innovation, and which are able to maintain the status quo of their business model, the higher cost and lock-in of a Cloud 1.0 solution may not present a severe limitation. Even though we are firmly of the opinion that businesses using on-premises and Cloud 1.0 solutions are anchoring themselves to the past.

For organizations that live and die based on their ability to innovate products, services, and business models, the choice of Cloud 2.0 and the eventual movement to the Bottomless Cloud is essential.

In this new framework, the business is built around the data. Data does not constrain the business model, but instead continuously shapes it and reshapes it to meet the demands of fast moving and rapidly evolving markets.

To be clear, we see the Bottomless Cloud as a mandatory rather than an optional change in the way data will be stored and managed, and how it will impact the success of every business.

The bottom line for every CEO, as we transition to this new era of data abundance, is that it's time to start considering how their businesses ability to compete is being enabled or constrained by the way that their organization's data is being stored and managed.

In the end, continuing to use a scarcity mindset to manage and leverage data will not only lag technology trends and competition, it will be downright negligent—as negligent as it would have been to continue using a water wheel to power a factory hoping to compete in the 20th century.

ASSESSMENT:
How Prepared Are You to Ask the
Right Questions About the Cloud?

The evolution of the Cloud is creating many questions that executives need to start asking. In the same way that a CEO would need to know the basic questions to ask in order to determine the financial and operational health of their organization, they also need to be ready to ask the right questions to determine how well it is leveraging the benefits of the Cloud. Here are two lists of questions that we suggest you ask of your organization. One set is for the business-focused c-level exec (CEO/CFO) and the other for the technology-focused c-level exec (CIO/CTO).

For the Business C-Level Exec:

What is the total monthly cost of your cloud data storage and how will it change over the next 12 months?

How much of your cloud data is available for immediate access?

What are the monthly usage costs of your cloud data?

What are the egress fees of moving your cloud data elsewhere?

What is the yearly rate of growth of your overall data storage?

What is the yearly rate of growth of your cloud data storage?

Do you know what your 2025 total cloud data storage requirements will be?

Have you factored in how disruptive technologies such as AI will impact your cloud data storage?

What percentage of your profitability can you directly link to your ability to apply data to new business models?

Does your cloud storage use a tiered architecture ranging from online to archived data? (If "Yes," then why?)

If your cloud storage doubled in size and access volumes, what would the impact be on your bottom line?

If you currently use a cloud data storage provider, does you stored data work with any cloud computing solution?

To what degree are you locked-in to your current cloud storage provider?

For the Technology C-Level Exec:

Is your data a core differentiator for the business?

Do you have a cloud data strategy that would be economically viable if your storage requirements doubled in the next 12 months?

Is your organization considering the use of AI technologies?

If "Yes," have you calculated the storage impact of AI?

What percentage of your overall IT spend is dedicated to data storage?

Is your data being used to support the development of new business models rather than just support legacy business?

When you think about how your data is currently used, would you consider yourself to be using an abundance or a scarcity model?

If your cloud data storage costs were reduced by 80%, what new business opportunities would arise?

If your cloud data retrieval speeds were increased by 1000%, what new business opportunities would arise?

Was your business built around data or is data a by-product of your business?

Notes

1. King, Hobart. "History of Energy Use in the United States." Geology. com. Retrieved November 11, 2018, from geology.com/articles/history-of-energy-use/.

2. O'Connor, Peter A. and Cleveland, Cutler J., (2014), U.S. Energy Transitions 1780–2010, Energies, 7, issue 12, p. 1-39, Retrieved November 11, 2018, from https://EconPapers.repec.org/RePEc:gam:jeners:v:7:y:2014:i:12:p:7955-7993:d:42829.

3. Ibid.

4. Mihm, S. (2018, March 5). How the U.S. Squandered Its Steel Superiority. Retrieved November 11, 2018, from bloomberg.com/opinion/articles/2018-03-05/steel-history-shows-how-america-lost-ground-to-europe.

5. Koulopoulos, T. M., & Roloff, T. M. (n.d.). *Smartsourcing*. (2006) Simon and Schuster.

6. Tom Bawden, "Global Warming: Data Centres to Consume Three Times as Much Energy in Next Decade, Experts Warn," *The Independent*, January 23, 2016, Retrieved on 11/11/2018 from http://www. independent.co.uk/environment/global-warming-data- centres-to-consume-three-times-as-much-energy-in-next- decade-experts-warn- a6830086.html.

7. Assumes Japan's current production of 979 terawatts/yr, its use of 7% of 416 terawatts of global data center power consumption or 30 terawatts, and doubling of data center power consumption every four years to equal approximately 150 terawatts by 2030. Does not assume potential costs savings from increased efficiency or production.

8. Press, G. (2016, August 8). IoT Mid-Year Update From IDC And Other Research Firms. Forbes. Retrieved November 11,2018, fromforbes.com/sites/gilpress/2016/08/05iot-mid-year-update-from-idc-and-other-research-firms/#748c180255c5.

9. Maddox, T. (2015, July 1). Research: 68% report cost is biggest data storage pain point. TechProResearch. Retrieved November 11, 2018, from techpro-research.com/article/research-68-report-cost-is-biggest-data-storage-pain-point/.

10. Anderson, C. (n.d.). *The Long Tail*. (2008) Random House.

11. Koulopoulos, T. M., & Roloff, T. M. (n.d.). *Smartsourcing*. (2006) Simon and Schuster.

12. Ibid.

13. Novet, J. (2018, February 1). Amazon cloud revenue jumps 45 percent in fourth quarter. CNBC. Retrieved November 11, 2018, from cnbc.com/2018/02/01/aws-earnings-q4-2017.html.

14. Alexis Madrigal. "How Netflix Reverse Engineered Hollywood," *The Atlantic*, January 2, 2014. Retrieved November 11, 2018.

https://www.theatlantic.com/technology/archive/2014/01/how-netflix-reverse-engineered-hollywood/282679/.

15. "How Netflix Uses Analytics To Select Movies, Create Content, and Make Multimillion Dollar Decisions," Kissmetrics (web log), accessed October 2, 2017, https://blog.kissmetrics.com/how-netflix-uses-analytics/.

16. Marr, B. (2016, November 15).How Nike And Under Armour Became Big Data Businesses. *Forbes*. Retrieved November 11, 2018, from forbes.com/sites/bernardmarr/2016/11/15/how-nike-and-under-armour-became-big-data-businesses/#2e2ebcd28669.

17. Dignan, L. (2015, December 4). Will Under Armour's big data, app experiment pay off? | ZDNet. ZDNet. Retrieved November 11, 2018, from zdnet.com/article/under-armours-grand-big-data-app-experiment-will-it-pay-off/.

18. Amend, James M. "Storage Almost Full: Driverless Cars Create Data Crunch." WardsAuto, 18 Jan. 2018, Retrieved November 11, 2018, wardsauto.com/technology/storage-almost-full-driverless-cars-create-data-crunch.

19. Peter Viechnicki, P. V., & William D. Eggers, W. E. (2017, April 26). How much time and money can AI save government? Retrieved November 11, 2018, from https://www2.deloitte.com/insights/us/en/focus/cognitive-technologies/artificial-intelligence-government-analysis.html.

20. Katie Allen, K. A. (2017, November 29). Technology has created more jobs than it has destroyed, says 140 years of data. Retrieved December 11, 2018, from https://www.theguardian.com/business/2015/aug/17/technology-created-more-jobs-than-destroyed-140-years-data-census.

21. Basel Kayyali, B. K., David Knott, D. K., & Steve Van Kuiken, S. K. (2013, January 30). The big-data revolution in US health care: Accelerating value and innovation. Retrieved December 11, 2018, from https://www.mckinsey.com/industries/healthcare-systems-and-services/our-insights/the-big-data-revolution-in-us-health-care.

22. Ibid.

23. Sebastian Anthony, S. A. (2012, August 17). Harvard cracks DNA storage, crams 700 terabytes of data into a single gram - ExtremeTech. Retrieved December 11, 2018, from http://www.extremetech.com/extreme/134672-harvard-cracks-dna-storage-crams-700-terabytes-of-data-into-a-single-gram.

24. Aviation depends on sensors and big data - News. (2017, November 1). Retrieved December 11, 2018, from https://siliconsemiconductor.net/article/102842/Aviation_Depends_On_Sensors_And_Big_Data%7BfeatureExtra%7D.

25. VNI Global Fixed and Mobile Internet Traffic Forecasts. (2018, November 27). Retrieved December 11, 2018, from https://www.cisco.com/c/en/us/solutions/service-provider/visual-networking-index-vni/index.html.

26. Koulopoulos, T. M. (2012). Cloud Surfing. Boston: Bibliomotion.

27. Ibid.

Just How Much Data Is That?

Kilobyte: 1 KB 10^3 = 1,000 Bytes
One page of double-spaced text

Megabyte: 1 MB 10^6 = 1,000,000 Bytes
One fairly lengthy book of 500 pages

Gigabyte: 1 GB 10^9 = 1,000,000,000 Bytes
All of the books in a small public school library

Terrabyte: 1 TB 10^{12} = 1,000,000,000,000 Bytes
10% of all the books cataloged in the US Library of Congress

Petabyte: 1 PB 10^{15} = 1,000 000 000 000 000 Bytes
1% of all the indexed pages on the World Wide web

Exabyte: 1 EB 10^{18} = 1,000,000,000,000,000,000 Bytes
Global Internet Traffic Hourly

Zettabyte: 1 ZB 10^{21} = 1,000,000,000,000,000,000,000 Bytes
Total Global Digital Data in 2017
(Also the diameter in meters of the MilkyWay)

Yottabyte: 1 YB 10^{24} = 1,000,000,000,000,000,000,000,000 Bytes
Total Global Digital Data Projected by 2035

(Also the number of stars in the observable universe)

Hellabyte: 1 HB 10^{27} = 1,000,000,000,000,000,000,000,000,000 Bytes

Total Global Digital Data Projected by 2050

(Also the number of nanoseconds—one billionth of a second—since the big bang)

Sexdecibyte*: 10^{51} Total number of atoms in the Earth

(Conservatively, the data storage requirements by 2200)

*There is no accepted name for this amount of storage, so we used the root that scientists use for the word that describes 10^{51}, sexdecillion.

David Friend

David Friend is the CEO and co-founder of Wasabi Technologies, his fifth tech start-up. Wasabi is ushering in a new generation of cloud storage solutions. Prior to Wasabi David co-founded Carbonite, one of the world's leading cloud backup companies. David graduated from Yale and was a David Sarnoff Fellow at Princeton. His first start-up, ARP Instruments, manufactured synthesizers for used by Stevie Wonder, Pete Townsend of the Who, Led Zeppelin, and dozens of others.

Tom Koulopoulos

Tom Koulopoulos is the Chairman and co-founder of Boston-based Delphi Group, a 30-year-old global futures think tank that focuses on the impact of digital technologies. Delphi Group was named one of the 500 fastest growing private companies in the US by *Inc* magazine. He is the author of 11 books, the past executive director of the Babson Center for Business Innovation, an adjunct professor at Boston University, and a frequent keynote speaker on the future.

Other books by Tom Koulopoulos:
Revealing The Invisible
The Gen Z Effect
Cloud Surfing
The Innovation Zone